a gift for:

_____

from:

_____

The Spirit of Hope
Copyright © 2007 Hallmark Licensing, Inc.

Published by Hallmark Books,
a division of Hallmark Cards, Inc.,
Kansas City, MO 64141
Visit us on the Web at www.Hallmark.com.

Editorial Director: Todd Hafer
Editor: Jeff Morgan
Art Director: Kevin Swanson
Designer: Michelle Nicolier
Illustrator: Cathy Johnson
Lettering Artist: Lisa Rogers
Production Artist: Dan Horton

ISBN: 978-1-59530-154-3
BOK5518

Printed and bound in China.

the spirit of

hope

GIFT BOOKS
from Hallmark

It is the nature of the world
to provide challenges.
It is human nature
to support one another
as we strive to overcome them.

Through challenges,
we grow braver,
become stronger,
emerge more confident than ever.

6

Bad things may happen to us, but they do not change who we are.

The journey of healing
takes patience and time,
love and support,
courage and hope.

Courage is doing what you must
when doing what you must
is the hardest thing of all.

Hope

quietly abides
in our souls
and whispers comfort
on our journeys
when we need it most.

Trouble lives its season,
shadows our hearts
until it is spent. It changes
the landscape, but leaves
a space for the light to return.

Even during the most troubled times, every once in a while, heaven breaks over the mountains to encourage us.

Flowers wait patiently for the sun to return,
knowing it always will.

Each sunrise reminds us that miracles happen.

Each drop of rain is a promise of growth.

Roots of courage yield blossoms of joy.

There is a quiet place
somewhere beyond tomorrow
where your heart will find peace
and the mists of troubles
will begin to clear away.

Sometimes the longer we sit
and listen to the quiet,
the more we come to know
our inner strengths.

Hope is the belief in things unseen.

33

Hope tucks itself
into the most unexpected places.

In the seed
is an apple
you can't yet see.

The apple tree itself,
if it ever found a voice,
could tell us
some things about life:
Bow to storms—
they will pass.
You can bend in the wind
without breaking.
You don't know how strong
you are until
your strength is tested.

Nurture your hopes.
Hold them close
and understand
that they are the seeds
of good things to come.

The pressures and problems
that sometimes surround us
are often defeated
by the courage and strength
that are always within us.

Even the strongest people must step back, take a deep breath, and summon their courage now and then.

Fear and worry are normal,
natural reactions to threats,
but so are courage and hope...
and they are the stronger,
the more enduring.

Though at times the story of your life is unsettled,
at its center there is the certainty of hope
and the promise of good things to come.

In the best stories there's a part
where the heroine decides
enough is enough. We love that part.

50

It's OK to tell whoever is raising
the high bar to give it a rest.

When you call on your strength
you find that place inside
that is free of stress
and home to a calm mind and spirit.

Trust.
Just be.
Take a risk.
Go back to bed.
Be still.
Watch mindless TV.
Eat extra dessert.
Take a hot bath.
Be amazing.
Believe.
Sleep in.
Have more chocolate.
Light a candle.
Rest.
Dream.
Hope.
Hold on.
Keep going.

57

Life happens.
Love helps.

60

The world is half as heavy
when two shoulder it together...

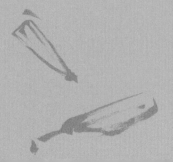

...and sometimes simply holding hands
is holding on to everything.

Trouble may run deep,
but love always runs deeper.

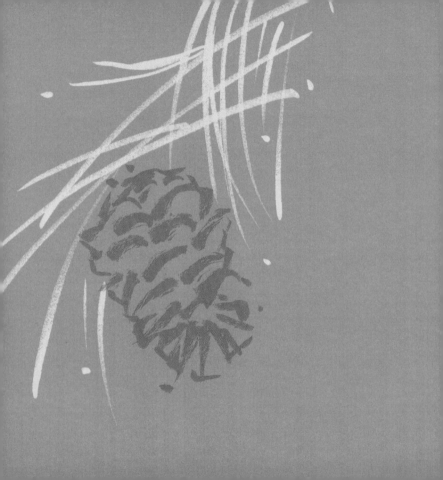

Just knowing that
we're cared about
can brighten even the dark
of the bleakest winter day.

Even in our winters,
there are bright days
that bring peaceful
and pleasant surprises.

Each hopeful moment
has a melody
all its own.

Believing is ninety percent of doing.

The stuff that wears on the nerves
polishes the soul.

Nothing is stronger than strength of spirit. The body may falter. But inside, unchanging, a spirit brilliant with strength and resilience shines on. And on. And on.

Dwell in possibilities.

Start where you are.
Use what you have.
Do what you can.

Horizons are made for going beyond.

83

Dreams come true one step

at a time.

You never know how far
you can go until you envision
a distant destination and
take the first steps.

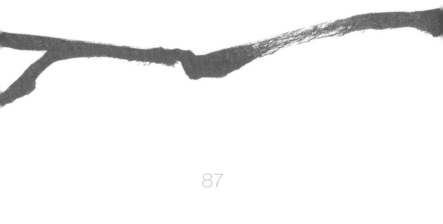

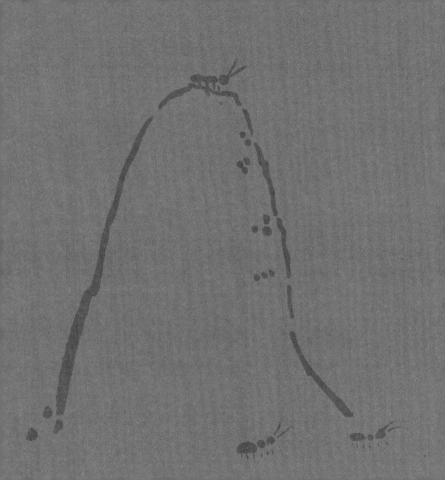

Even a well-planned journey
can have a rough road now and then…

...but somewhere down that road,
there's a smooth lake.

Adversity rewrites the stories
of our lives, changes the cast
of characters, and alters
what we expected would happen.
Yet the stories go on and someday,
behind the scenes, we'll find
the true importance
of their twists and turns.

Deep inside us, we have a spirit
of energy and determination,
a spirit that refuses to be broken —
and we call this hope. Even when
life's challenges overwhelm us
our hope inspires us to rise
to new heights.

No one knows the challenge
better than you. Advice is fine,
but trust your own instincts,
follow your heart. And keep on
keeping on, little by little,
one day at a time.

All you've got
is all you can give
and that will always be enough.

We'd love to hear from you
if you have enjoyed this book.

Please send your comments to:
Book Feedback Mail Drop 215
2501 McGee, Kansas City, MO 64108
or email us at
booknotes@hallmark.com